PRECIOUS EARTH

Saving Oceans and Wetlands

Jen Green

Chrysalis Education

Distributed in the United States by
Smart Apple Media
1980 Lookout Drive
North Mankato, Minnesota 56003

Copyright © Chrysalis Books Group Plc 2004

Library of Congress Control Number: 2003116151

ISBN 1-59389-139-3

Editorial Manager: Joyce Bentley

Produced by
Tall Tree Ltd.
Designer: Ed Simkins
Editor: Kate Simkins
Consultant: Michael Rand
Picture Researcher: Lorna Ainger

Printed in Hong Kong

Some of the more unfamiliar words used in this book
are explained in the glossary on page 31.

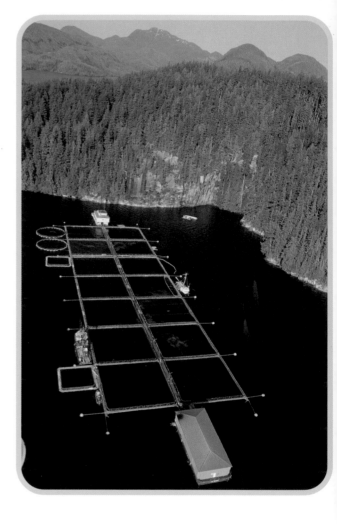

Contents

Watery planet

Water covers over 70 percent of our planet's surface. Almost all of that is salty ocean. Only a tiny fraction is freshwater found in wetlands (rivers, lakes, streams, and marshes), at the polar ice caps, and among rocks underground.

Water is vital to all living things on Earth. Indeed, life began in the oceans billions of years ago. Since prehistoric times, people have settled by oceans and wetlands, fishing for food and traveling by boat. Wetlands also provide water for drinking, farming and, in the last few hundred years, for industry, too.

▼ *The Pacific Ocean is the world's largest ocean, covering about half of the Earth's surface.*

For centuries, people have also used oceans and wetlands to dump sewage and other garbage. Until recently, people believed that the oceans were so huge that this would not cause problems. Now scientists have discovered that the waters are slowly being poisoned by waste.

◀ Polluted water from a factory pours into a river in Germany. Many of the world's wetlands are now badly polluted by waste from industry.

CLOSE TO HOME

Seawater is salty because it contains minerals washed from the land by rivers. The most common minerals are sodium and chlorine, which together make salt. Next time you swim in the sea, notice how the water leaves behind a white powder (the salt) as it dries on your skin.

The water cycle

Oceans and wetlands play a vital role in many natural cycles on Earth that allow life to flourish. For example, they bring life-giving rain to the land.

Water moves constantly between the air, oceans, and land in a journey called the water cycle. As the Sun's heat warms the surface of seas and lakes, it produces a gas called water vapor.
This gas rises to form clouds made of tiny water drops. In the clouds, the water drops combine into bigger drops, which fall as rain. The rain eventually flows back into the sea.

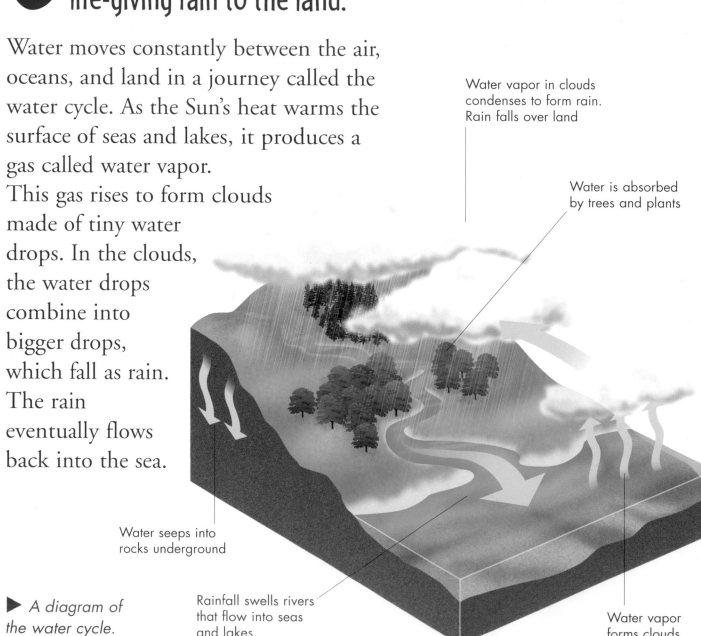

Water vapor in clouds condenses to form rain. Rain falls over land

Water is absorbed by trees and plants

Water seeps into rocks underground

▶ *A diagram of the water cycle.*

Rainfall swells rivers that flow into seas and lakes

Water vapor forms clouds

Seawater is never still but is constantly swirled by waves, tides, and currents. Ocean currents are driven by differences in water temperature. Warm currents from tropical areas heat places such as Western Europe. Elsewhere, cold currents from polar seas cool the land. In this way, ocean currents help to spread the Sun's heat around the globe.

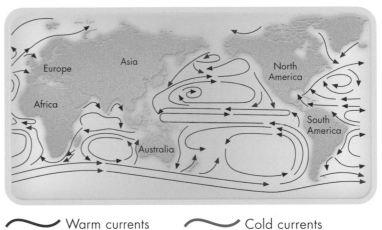

~ Warm currents   ~ Cold currents

Wet winds blowing off the ocean bring rain to coasts. The oceans also absorb the Sun's heat more slowly than the land but hold it for longer. This means that sea breezes cool the land in summer and warm it in winter, creating a mild climate.

▼ *Lands affected by ocean breezes have mild, wet weather, called a maritime climate. This coast is in Wales, United Kingdom.*

Aquatic life

Oceans and wetlands contain a greater variety of life than almost any place on land. All aquatic life is linked because each animal depends on other living things for food.

Aquatic animals depend on plants or other animals to survive. Plants trap and store the Sun's energy to make their own food. This energy is passed on to animals that eat the plants and passed on again to animals that eat the plant-eating animals. This is called a food chain. A simple ocean food chain could begin with the microscopic plants called plankton and end with a large predator, like a shark.

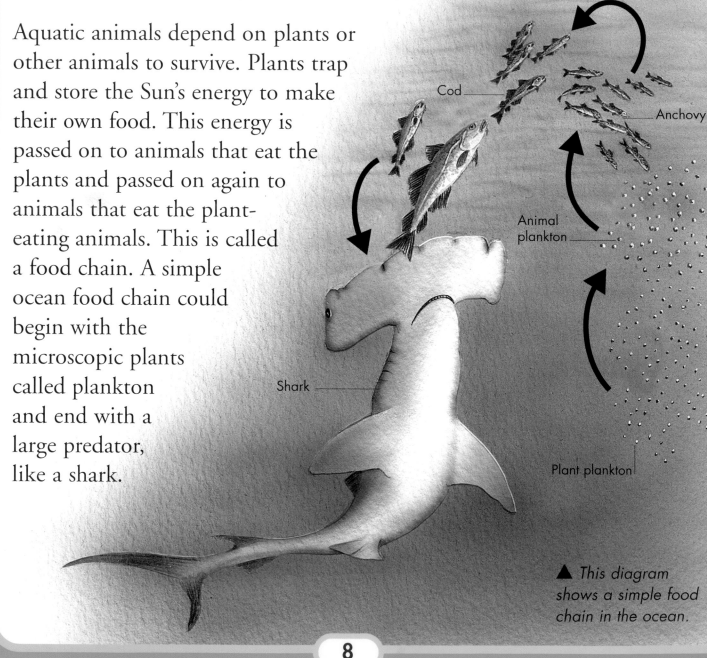

Cod

Anchovy

Animal plankton

Shark

Plant plankton

▲ *This diagram shows a simple food chain in the ocean.*

Plants and animals thrive in the upper sunlit waters of the oceans, where it is warmer and food is plentiful. As the oceans become deeper and darker, fewer creatures can survive the harsh conditions. Many creatures live in shallow waters around coral reefs like this one.

▼ *Wetland animals are also linked in food chains. This heron is feeding on a fish.*

Oceans and wetlands contain many different habitats. Each habitat is home to different creatures. In the oceans, these habitats include rocky shores, sandy shores, coral reefs, and estuaries. They also include the different depths of water, from the sunlit surface down to the dark ocean floor. Wetland habitats include rushing streams, slow-moving rivers, still lakes, ponds, marshes, and bogs. Each type of habitat has its own unique plants and animals.

Using the oceans

Oceans have provided people with food and a means of transportation since prehistoric times. For thousands of years, people have been sailing the seas to hunt fish and other marine life and to get from place to place.

In early times, fishermen used spears and simple hooks. Over many centuries, fishing methods became much more efficient. Huge nets as well as new techniques, such as sonar, now help fishing fleets to catch so many fish that few are left to breed. In the 20th century, so many whales were killed that they, too, became scarce.

▼ *Fish are a major source of food worldwide. Some fish that were once common, such as cod, are now rare, because so many have been caught.*

There are many other uses for the oceans. People drill for oil and gas and dredge minerals, such as copper and nickel, from the seabed. A process known as desalination produces freshwater from seawater. People also travel to the sea for vacation.

▲ Oil rigs like this one in Canada are used to drill for oil and gas on the seabed. Around 25 percent of the oil and gas we use is now mined offshore.

CLOSE TO HOME

Most of us enjoy seafoods, such as shrimp. However, the sea also provides many other useful foods. Seaweed can be used to thicken a variety of foods, including gelatin. Sea salt is used to flavor and preserve food. Some marine plants and animals are also used in medicines.

Ocean pollution

A staggering 22 billion tons of garbage are dumped in the oceans each year. The waste pollutes the clear waters and harms marine plants and animals.

Oil sometimes pollutes the oceans. Oil spills into the sea when oil tankers are involved in accidents. In 1989, the tanker *Exxon Valdez* hit a reef off Alaska. Over 10 million gallons of oil spilled into the water. Many thousands of fish, shellfish, seabirds, and otters died.

▲ *After the Exxon Valdez oil spill, floating booms were used to try to stop the oil from spreading, but 1,250 miles of coastline were still affected.*

Sewage is used water from homes, factories, and farms that contains human waste and chemicals. Some of this water is cleaned and reused (see page 19). The rest ends up in the sea. Highly poisonous waste from nuclear power plants is sometimes dumped at sea.

▼ *This map shows the parts of the oceans that are most polluted. Coastal waters are often the worst hit.*

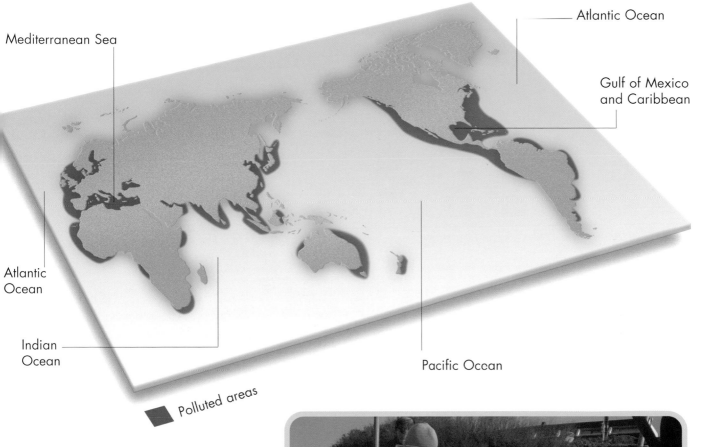

Mediterranean Sea

Atlantic Ocean

Gulf of Mexico and Caribbean

Atlantic Ocean

Indian Ocean

Pacific Ocean

■ Polluted areas

CLOSE TO HOME

Garbage and sewage pollute many beaches around the world. People can even get sick after swimming in the water. Sometimes, volunteers help clean up local beaches.

Other dangers

As well as dumping at sea, pollution from the air and land is also harming the oceans. Air pollution, for example, is making the weather warmer, which affects sea levels.

Global warming is a worldwide problem that is affecting the oceans. Cars, factories, and power plants release waste gases, as they burn coal, oil, and gas. These gases trap the Sun's heat, making the weather warmer. As the temperature of the oceans rises, so the water expands to cause flooding. In the polar regions, the ice caps are melting, causing sea levels to rise.

▼ *This family escaped by raft when floods hit the low-lying country of Bangladesh in Asia in 2000. Floods like this are becoming more common, partly because of global warming.*

Scientists fear that global warming is also upsetting the world's weather. Hurricanes are huge tropical storms that form over warm seas and cause great destruction when they reach land. As the seas heat up because of global warming, devastating hurricanes are becoming more common.

▶ *This damage in Florida in 1998 was caused by a hurricane.*

LOOK CLOSER

In 1998, the Coto Doñana National Park in Spain was poisoned by waste from a mine upriver when a dam burst. Small creatures, such as worms and shellfish, absorbed the waste. They were eaten by larger creatures and so the poison spread up the food chain. These fish died after eating poisoned food.

Shallow seas

The shallow waters around islands, coral reefs, and coasts are rich in wildlife. However, nature is delicately balanced in these places and so is easily disturbed.

Some islands contain plants and animals found nowhere else. This is because island wildlife has adapted to suit its habitat. For example, some island birds, such as the kakapo of New Zealand, cannot fly because they never needed to escape hunters. When Europeans arrived and brought cats, flightless kakapos were easily caught by these new predators.

▼ Marine iguanas are seagoing lizards found only on the Galapagos Islands off South America. They are threatened by the arrival of new animals on the islands, including cats and rats.

In warm, shallow seas, coral reefs are home to an amazing variety of sea life. However, these delicate reefs are now threatened by overfishing, sewage, and warming seas. Around the world, some coasts are also being harmed by industry, farming, or growing numbers of tourists. Vacationers drop litter and disturb wildlife.

◀ *An unspoiled coral reef in the Caribbean. Divers sometimes harm beautiful reefs like this by breaking off pieces of coral to take home as souvenirs.*

LOOK CLOSER

Sea turtles lay their eggs on beaches. When the babies hatch, they head for the safety of the ocean. On beaches now lit by hotels, some young turtles get confused and head for the bright lights instead. They don't reach the safety of the ocean and are soon killed by predators.

Wetlands

The world's wetlands include rivers, lakes, ponds, swamps, bogs, and salty estuaries, where rivers meet the sea. Wetlands shelter all kinds of wildlife, not just freshwater animals, but also young sea creatures and migrating birds.

Thousands of years ago, the first settlements grew up by rivers and other wetlands. Today, many of the world's greatest cities lie on riverbanks. Wetlands provide water to drink and food like fish, shrimp, crabs, and waterfowl. Crops, including wheat and rice, are grown in fields watered by rivers and lakes.

▼ Fish and shellfish from the wetlands are caught and sold in faraway cities. In Botswana in Africa, boys catch fish using baskets made from reeds.

As well as food and water, wetlands have many other uses. For example, they provide gravel and sand for building and peat for fertilizer and fuel. Valuable minerals, such as gold, are sometimes found in rivers. Lakes, swamps, and bogs soak up moisture after heavy rains and so help to prevent floods.

▲ Wetlands are very important for transportation. Flat-bottomed barges are used to carry goods along rivers, such as the Mississippi.

CLOSE TO HOME

Much of the water we drink comes from rivers, other wetlands, and reservoirs. In rich countries, it is carefully cleaned and tested to make sure it is safe. Wastewater from homes passes through sewage plants that filter it and then return it to wetlands. In big cities, drinking water may have been cleaned and reused over a dozen times.

Harming wetlands

Today, many of the world's wetlands are in trouble because of pollution. Sewage and chemicals from farms and factories spill into the water and poison wildlife.

In rich countries, many farmers use chemical fertilizers on their fields to increase the harvest. When these chemicals leak into rivers after rainfall, they cause bacteria and tiny plants called algae to breed very quickly. These block out the light and use up much of the oxygen needed for other plants and animals.

▼ Green algae blanket the surface of a river in Italy. Fish and other wildlife below are starved of oxygen and light.

Factories also produce pollution that is harming wetlands. Factory chimneys give off chemicals that mix with water vapor in the air to form acid rain. This kills trees, then drains off into wetlands to poison aquatic life. Some factories also empty harmful chemicals directly into rivers.

▲ *Waste from a copper mine has polluted this river in Spain. The waste is colored and so the damage is easily seen.*

CLOSE TO HOME

In rich countries, wastewater from homes passes to the water treatment plant (shown here). There it is filtered to remove sewage, chemicals, and other pollutants and returned to the river. Next time you take a shower, think about where the wastewater goes.

Threatened wetlands

Around the world, wetlands and their wildlife are disappearing quickly as people build dams and drain marshes. The United States has lost about half of all its wetlands in the few hundred years since European settlers arrived.

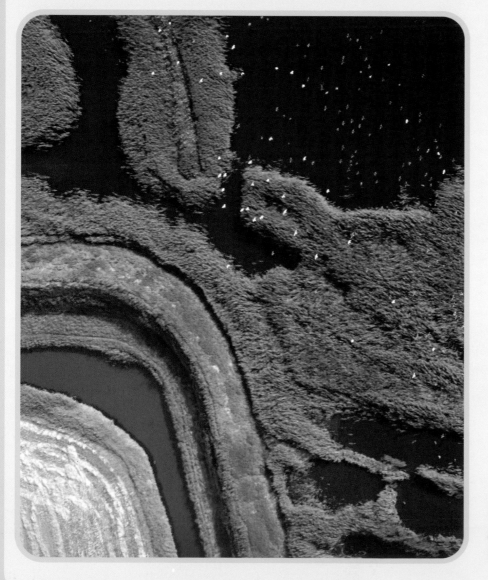

Wetlands are often drained to provide new land for farming or to build on. In hot countries, marshes are sometimes cleared to control mosquitoes, which breed there and spread disease.

◄ *Wetlands by the sea were drained to make this farmland in the Netherlands.*

Wetlands are also harmed when large dams are built. Dams destroy wildlife and can also disturb people's lives. Egyptian farmers once relied on the yearly flooding of the Nile River to make their fields fertile (the water brought with it nutrient-rich mud). A large dam built in the 1960s stopped the flooding. The farmers now use chemical fertilizers instead.

▼ *The Three Gorges Dam is a huge dam project now being built in China to supply electricity. The dam will flood 10 major towns, and all the people who live there will have to move.*

The Aral Sea in Asia was once a huge body of water fed by two rivers. Fishermen fished the sea, and farmers grew crops nearby. In the 1960s, the rivers that ran into the sea were diverted to water other land. As the sea dried up, the remaining water became too salty to drink or to irrigate crops. Farms and the local fishing industry were destroyed.

Taking action

In recent years, more and more people have become concerned about the damage that is being done to oceans and wetlands. Governments and wildlife organizations are now working to tackle these problems.

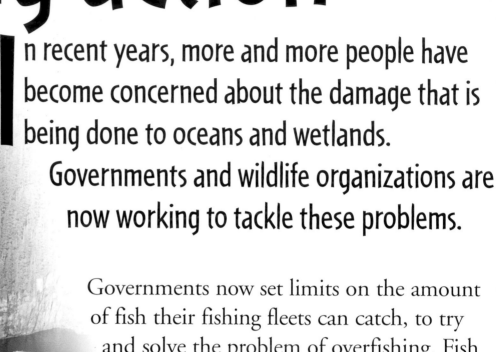

Governments now set limits on the amount of fish their fishing fleets can catch, to try and solve the problem of overfishing. Fish farming—the rearing of fish and shellfish in sheltered pens—can also help to save wild marine life. Meanwhile, some wetlands that were drained have been restored to their original condition. Other areas now enjoy official protection as reserves and national parks.

◀ *Salmon are being reared on this fish farm in Canada.*

▶ *These campaigners are protesting about the many dolphins that drown when they get caught in fishermen's nets by accident. The sign reads "Death by drowning."*

LOOK CLOSER

Some parts of the oceans and wetlands have been made into sanctuaries to protect wildlife. Tourists, such as these whale watchers, can visit to enjoy the scenery and wildlife. Tourism helps pay for the reserve, but it is a delicate balance, since too many tourists can disturb the wildlife.

In the last 30 years, campaigns by protest groups, such as Greenpeace, have helped to save whales, seals, and other sea creatures. These groups have also fought to stop the dumping of dangerous waste. In response, many governments have now passed laws to protect rare creatures and control pollution. Protesters have also helped to stop the building of several large dams that would have harmed wetlands.

How can we help?

We can all help to protect oceans, wetlands, and their wildlife. For example, always take your litter away with you (and recycle it!) after you visit the seaside.

The amount of water we use at home puts a strain on local reservoirs and wild wetlands. Try to use water carefully—for example, don't leave faucets running and take showers instead of baths. Using small amounts of soap or detergents that are kind to the environment helps to reduce the pollution of wetlands.

◄ *Save water in the garden by using watering cans filled with rainwater to water plants instead of a hose.*

Saving energy helps to reduce the pollution that is leading to global warming. It's easy—just switch off lights and other machines when they're not needed. You could also join an organization that works to protect local wildlife.

◀ Ask your teacher if you can organize a class trip to the local beach or river to clean up litter. Wear gloves and always take care near water.

Some seaside shops sell souvenirs made from sea creatures, such as sharks' teeth, pieces of coral, and shells. Wild creatures are sometimes killed to make these trinkets, so do not to buy them unless you are sure they have not been collected in this way. Never disturb animals, such as seabirds or turtles, on the beach.

▼ Hawksbill turtles are now very rare because they have been hunted for their beautiful shells, which are used to make souvenirs.

Oceans projects

Your nearest seashore contains several mini-habitats for wildlife. Find out more about the plants and animals that live there. The tracks of birds or mammals on the beach or riverbank provide clues about how these animals live.

BEACH DETECTIVE

If you look closely at your nearest beach, you will find that there are all kinds of living creatures.

Keep a notebook or journal with your observations about the beach. Is the beach rocky, sandy, or shingly? On sandy beaches, worms, shellfish, and crabs lurk in burrows, leaving telltale holes in the sand. Rocky beaches are rich in wildlife. Rockpools are mini-habitats with a wide variety of creatures that can live in and out of the water. Look for anemones, seasnails, shrimp, crabs, and fish.

▲ Look closely for creatures in a rockpool. If you have a net, you can use it to fish out small creatures (but always put them back). Take an adult with you.

LOOKING AT TRACKS

Birds, mammals, and other animals often leave clear tracks in the wet mud of riverbanks, by the edge of ponds, or on sandy beaches. Use a book about local wildlife to identify the prints you find. Always take an adult with you when you visit locations near water.

▶ If you can't make a plaster cast, draw the animal track instead.

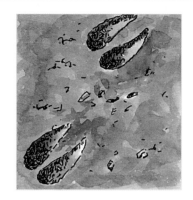

1. The tracks of ducks, geese, moorhens, deer, and voles are often seen by the river. Gulls, wading birds, ponies, and crabs may leave prints on the seashore.

2. You can make a cast of the tracks you find using plaster of Paris. First place a plastic or cardboard ring around the print. Slowly add water to some plaster of Paris in a bowl, mixing it to make a stiff paste.

3. Pour the mixture on, then leave it to dry for 20 minutes. Carefully dig up the cast using a trowel or beach shovel. Leave the cast to dry thoroughly for a day, then clean and decorate it using poster paints.

CAMPAIGN GROUPS

Friends of the Earth
1025 Vermont Ave., NW, Suite 300, Washington, D.C. 20005

Greenpeace
702 H Street, NW, Suite 300
Washington, D.C. 20001

World Wildlife Fund
1250 24th Street, NW
Washington, D.C.
20037-1175

OCEANS AND WETLANDS WEBSITES

US Fish and Wildlife Service: endangered.fws.gov/kids/how_help.htm

The Coral Reef Alliance: www.coral.org

Environmental Investigation Agency: www.eia-international.org

Marine Conservation Society: www.mcsuk.org

World Conservation Monitoring Center: www.unep-wcmc.org

Other good sites: www.kidsplanet.org

www.endangeredspecie.com/kids.htm

Surfers Against Sewage: www.sas.org.uk

Oceans factfile

- In the last 30 years, there have been several major oil spills as large as the *Exxon Valdez* spill. For example, when the oil tanker *Sea Empress* was holed off Wales, United Kingdom, in 1996, 80,000 tons of oil spilled into the sea.

- In the 1950s, the total catch made by the world's fishermen was about 15.5 million tons of fish. By 1990, the total catch was over 77 million tons. So many fish were caught that numbers of some fish have fallen steeply since.

- Fish farms now supply 4.4 million tons of fish annually.

- The world's largest coral reef is the Great Barrier Reef off Australia. It stretches for over 1,250 miles and is a World Heritage Site, which means that wildlife there is protected.

- By the 1980s, many types of whales had become scarce through overhunting. In 1988, almost all nations agreed to stop hunting whales.

- In the future, we may be able to harness the power of waves and tides to generate electricity. The technology involved is expensive at the moment and needs to be developed.

Glossary

Acid rain
Rain that is more acidic than normal because it contains pollution from factories.

Aquatic
Aquatic plants, animals, and other living things dwell in water.

Algae
Tiny simple plants that grow in water or damp places.

Climate
The regular pattern of weather in a particular place.

Condense
To change from a gas into a liquid.

Global warming
Warming weather worldwide, caused by the increase of gases in the air that trap the Sun's heat near the planet's surface.

Habitat
A place where certain types of plants and animals live, such as a river estuary or a coral reef.

Irrigate
To supply land with water using pipes or channels, usually to grow crops.

Marine
Belonging to the sea.

Nutrient
A substance that is full of goodness and is absorbed by the roots of plants.

Overfishing
When so many fish are caught that not enough remain to breed, so that fish become scarce.

Plankton
The microscopic plants and animals that float at the surface of oceans and lakes.

Predator
An animal that hunts other animals for food.

Reservoir
An artificial lake made to hold water.

Sewage
Dirty water from homes and factories, that contains chemicals and human waste.

Wetland
Any body of freshwater, including streams, rivers, lakes, ponds, marshes, and bogs. Salty estuaries are where rivers meet the sea.

Index